W9-BXN-328

First Facts®

PREDATOR PROFILES

HYENAS

– BUILT FOR THE HUNT –

by Tammy Gagne

Consultant: Dr. Jackie Gai, DVM
Wildlife Veterinarian

Peachtree
CAPSTONE PRESS
a capstone imprint

First Facts are published by Capstone Press,
1710 Roe Crest Drive, North Mankato, Minnesota 56003
www.mycapstone.com

Library of Congress Cataloging-in-Publication Data
Gagne, Tammy, author.
Hyenas : built for the hunt / by Tammy Gagne.
pages cm.—(First facts. Predator profiles)
Audience: Ages 6-9.
Audience: K to grade 3.
Summary: "Describes the features, behaviors, and adaptations that make hyenas skilled
predators"—Provided by publisher.
Includes bibliographical references and index.
ISBN 978-1-4914-8259-9 (library binding)
ISBN 978-1-4914-8261-2 (eBook PDF)
1. Hyenas—Juvenile literature. 2. Predation (Biology)—Juvenile literature. I. Title.
QL737.C24G34 2016
599.74'3—dc23   2015020220

Editorial Credits
Carrie Braulick Sheely, editor; Sarah Bennett and Juliette Peters, designers;
Tracy Cummins, media researcher; Tori Abraham, production specialist

Photo Credits
FLPA: Lacz, 6 Bottom; Getty Images: Per-Gunnar Ostby, 11; iStockphoto: Angelika Stern,
8, mit4711, 19, WLDavies, 13; Minden Pictures: Anup Shah, 5; Shutterstock: Albie Venter,
12, Anan Kaewkhammul, 6 Middle Left, bonga1965, 18, EcoPrint, 6 Middle Right, Erwin
Niemand, 15, gualtiero boffi, 6 Top, Johan Swanepoel, 17, Nachaliti, Cover, Peter Schwarz,
9, rujithai, 3, Stacey Ann Alberts, 2, Sue Berry, Cover Back, Tamer Desouky, 1; SuperStock:
Biosphoto, 21; Thinkstock: Anup Shah, 14

Printed and bound in China.
007479LEOS16

TABLE OF CONTENTS

STRENGTH IN NUMBERS

Hyenas aren't the biggest animals in Africa. The largest hyenas are only about 2.5 feet (0.8 meter) tall. But don't let their size fool you. These animals are powerful **predators**. A group of spotted hyenas can take down animals three times their own size.

FACT

Spotted hyenas work together when hunting **herd** animals such as zebras. These hyenas usually hunt in groups of three to five. But they may form larger groups.

predator—an animal that hunts other animals for food

herd—a large group of animals that lives or moves together

PREDATORS WITH A PLAN

Hyenas usually attack a young or weak member of a herd. One hyena rushes into the group to **distract** the other animals. The remaining hyenas work on cutting the target off from the herd. Once they have the **prey** alone, the hyenas attack. After a kill is made, hyenas often fight over the **carcass**.

spotted hyena

striped hyena

distract—to draw attention to something else

prey—an animal hunted by another animal for food

carcass—the body of a dead animal

species—a group of animals with similar features

HYENA SPECIES

There are four hyena **species**. They include the spotted hyena, striped hyena, and brown hyena. The aardwolf is also a member of the hyena family. However, its hunting habits and diet are very different from those of the other species.

brown hyena

aardwolf

Species	Hunting Habits	What It Eats	Where It Lives
Spotted Hyena	alone or in groups	wildebeest, zebras, antelope, gazelles, lizards, rabbits, foxes, birds, warthogs, sheep, goats, animals already dead	Africa
Striped Hyena	mainly alone	birds, lizards, rabbits, sheep, goats, insects, fruit, animals already dead	Africa, Asia
Brown Hyena	alone or in small groups	birds, rodents, lizards, insects, fruit, eggs, animals already dead	Africa
Aardwolf	alone	mainly termites	Africa

WHATEVER IT TAKES

Spotted hyenas are the largest hyena species. They kill at least three-quarters of their own food. These hyenas hunt wildebeest, zebras, gazelles, and warthogs. Other species eat smaller animals, such as mice, rabbits, and even bugs.

Hyenas are also **scavengers**. They eat meat other predators have left behind.

FACT

Hyenas sometimes try to steal the kills of lions. But in western Africa, lions have been seen eating the kills of hyenas. Prey can be hard to find in the area.

scavenger—an animal that feeds on animals that are already dead

OUTRUNNING PREY

Hyenas use their speed and **stamina** to hunt. When racing after zebras and other fast prey, spotted hyenas can run up to 37 miles (60 kilometers) per hour. They can keep running for up to 3 miles (5 km) at 25 to 31 miles (40 to 50 km) per hour.

stamina—the ability to keep doing an activity for long periods of time

CRUSHING JAWS

Hyenas use their sharp teeth and powerful jaws to kill prey. A spotted hyena's bite is as strong as a lion's. Most predators eat only the meat from their kills. But hyenas eat the bones, teeth, and even hooves of their prey!

FACT

Hyenas can **digest** the bones and teeth of the animals they eat. But a hyena will often throw up any hooves or horns it eats.

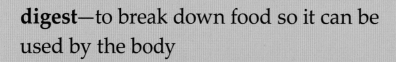

digest—to break down food so it can be used by the body

SHARP SENSES

Hyenas hunt at night. They depend on their sharp eyesight and hearing to find prey in the dark. But it's their sense of smell that sets hyenas apart from most other African predators. Their noses can pick up the scent of a carcass up to 2.5 miles (4 km) away.

FACT

Hyenas also find carcasses by watching for **vultures** flying overhead. The hyenas then follow the birds to the food.

vulture—a large bird that eats dead animals and has a featherless head

ONE ON ONE

Spotted hyenas usually hunt in groups. Brown and striped hyenas often hunt small animals alone. But spotted hyenas can take down big animals on their own. One spotted hyena can easily take down a lone springbok. This African gazelle can weigh nearly as much as the hyena.

FACT

Hyenas are related to cats. But they do not **stalk** prey like cats do. Instead, hyenas depend on their speed to outrun the animals.

stalk—to hunt slowly and quietly

A brown hyena carries off its prey.

MEALS ON THE RUN

Hyenas defend their kills from other predators. But they seem to know when the odds are against them. When hyenas are losing the fight, they will run away. But before they do, they often tear off a large chunk of meat from the kill.

FACT

Spotted hyenas make more than 11 different sounds.

MINE!

As many as 80 hyenas may live in groups called clans. In these clans, hyenas have a social rank. The leaders eat first. Other members may have to fight to get part of a kill.

Spotted hyenas are not in danger of dying out. But numbers of other hyena species are declining. People continue to watch hyenas' numbers. The predators are an important part of African **ecosystems**.

AMAZING BUT TRUE!

Because hyenas don't always eat every day, they may **gorge** themselves when they make a large kill. A single hyena can eat 33 pounds (15 kilograms) of meat at one feeding. That's like a person eating about 132 quarter-pound hamburgers in a single sitting!

ecosystem—a group of animals and plants that work together with their surroundings

gorge—to eat greedily

GLOSSARY

carcass (KAHR-kuhs)—the dead body of an animal

digest (dy-JEST)—to break down food so it can be used by the body

distract (dis-TRAKT)—to draw attention to something else

ecosystem (EE-koh-sis-tuhm)—a group of animals and plants that work together with their surroundings

gorge (GORJ)—to eat greedily

herd (HURD)—a large group of animals that lives or moves together

predator (PRED-uh-ter)—an animal that hunts other animals for food

prey (PRAY)—an animal hunted by another animal for food

scavenger (SKAV-uhn-jer)—an animal that feeds on animals that are already dead

species (SPEE-sheez)—a group of animals with similar features

stalk (STAWK)—to hunt slowly and quietly

stamina (STAM-uh-nuh)—the ability to keep doing an activity for long periods of time

vulture (VUHL-cher)—a large bird that eats dead animals and has a featherless head

READ MORE

O'Mara, Kennon. *Hunting with Hyenas.* When Animals Attack! New York: Gareth Stevens Publishing, 2014.

Schuetz, Kari. *Hyenas.* Blastoff! Readers: Animal Safari. Bellwether Media, 2012.

Quinlan, Julia J. *Hyenas.* Ferocious Fighting Animals. New York: PowerKids Press, 2013.

INTERNET SITES

FactHound offers a safe, fun way to find Internet sites related to this book. All of the sites on FactHound have been researched by our staff.

Here's all you do:

Visit *www.facthound.com*

Type in this code: 9781491482599

Check out projects, games and lots more at
www.capstonekids.com

CRITICAL THINKING
USING THE COMMON CORE

1. Look at the chart on page 7. Explain one way the hyena species are different from one another. Explain one way they are the same. (Craft and Structure)

2. Name a sense hyenas have and explain how it helps them hunt. (Key Ideas and Details)

INDEX